Handwriting

by

George

Rules of Civility
&
Decent Behavior

To Draw & Write
In Company and conversation
Rules 1-27

Greenleaf Press,
Lebanon , TN

www.greenleafpress.com
1570 Old Laguardo Rd
Lebanon, TN 37087
GReenLeaf
P·R·E·S·S

Introduction
and notes for parents & teachers

When George Washington was sixteen years old, he began copying 110 maxims for polite behavior into his schoolbooks. These rules describe the behavior of a gentleman, and many claim that they greatly influenced Washington's attitudes and standards for his own behavior.

*Several years ago we became aware of George Washington's **Rules of Decency and Civility**. We were all tired of the standard handwriting practice book copy material and began using Washington's **Rules** as copy work. While many of them may seem at first only to have application to the eighteenth century, they also have a lot to say to modern gentlemen and ladies. We hadn't expected to enjoy these sayings as much as we did. They rarely stayed merely copywork exercise but became the basis of other discussions. "Show nothing to your friend that might affright him," became a part of a discussion about why the children should not torment our guests (particularly the one with the intense mouse phobia) with the dead mouse discovered under the sink. Other rules addressed issues involving putting others first and self last - and other ways to show respect to those around us.*

In this book, we have included rules 1-27, with other volumes to follow that will complete the set. For each rule, there is space to copy it at least once, and space to draw an illustration. Be sure to talk about the ways you can apply the rule to your relationships with those around you. Enjoy!

Cyndy Shearer

Note: The **Rules** have been typeset using a D'Nealian style font designed by Donald Thurber. For a summary of the advantages of teaching handwriting using this style, visit www.dnealian.com

Rule 1

Every action done in company ought to be with some sign of respect to those that are present.

Rule 2

When in company, put not your hands to any part of the body not usually discovered.

Rule 3

Show nothing to your friend that may affright him.

Rule 4

In the presence of others, sing not to yourself with a humming noise, nor drum with your fingers or feet.

Rule 5

If you cough, sneeze, sigh, or yawn, do it not loud but privately; and speak not in your yawning, but put your handkerchief or hand before your face and turn aside.

Rule 6

Sleep not when others speak, sit not when others stand, speak not when you should hold your peace, walk not when others stop.

Rule 7

Put not off your clothes in the presence of others, nor go out of your chambers half dressed.

Rule 8

At play and at fire it is good manners to give place to the last comer, and affect not to speak louder than ordinary.

Rule 9

Spit not in the fire, nor stoop low before it. Neither put your hand into the flames to warm them, nor set your feet upon the fire, especially if there be meat before it.

Rule 10

When you sit down, keep your feet firm and even, without putting one on the other or crossing them.

Rule 11

Shift not yourself in the sight of others nor gnaw your nails.

Rule 12

Shake not the head, feet, or legs; roll not the eyes;
lift not one eyebrow higher than the other; wry not the
mouth; and bedew no man's face with your spittle by
approaching too near him when you speak.

Rule 13

Kill no vermin as fleas, lice, and ticks in the sight of others; if you see any filth or thick spittle, put your foot dexterously upon it; if it be upon the clothes of your companions, put if off privately; and if it be upon your own clothes, return thanks to him who puts it off.

Rule 14

Turn not your back to others especially in speaking; jog not the table or desk on which another reads or writes; lean not upon anyone.

Rule 15

Keep your nails clean and short, also your hands and teeth clean, yet without showing any great concern for them.

Rule 16

Do not puff up the cheeks; loll not out the tongue, rub the hands, or beard, thrust out the lips, or bite them, or keep the lips too open or closed.

Rule 17

Be no flatterer, neither play with any that delights not to be played with.

Rule 18

Read no letters, books, or papers in company; but when there is a necessity for the doing of it, you must ask leave. Come not near the books or writings of another so as to read them unless desired or give your opinion of them unasked; also look not nigh when another is writing a letter.

Rule 19

Let your countenance be pleasant, but in serious matters somewhat grave.

Rule 20

The gestures of the body must be suited to the discourse you are upon.

Rule 21

Reproach none for the infirmities of nature, nor delight to put them that have in mind thereof.

Rule 22

Show not yourself glad at the misfortune of another, though he were your enemy.

Rule 23

When you see a crime punished, you may be inwardly pleased, but always show pity to the suffering offender.

Rule 24

Do not laugh too much or too loud at any public spectacle.

Rule 25

Superfluous compliments and all affectation of ceremony are to be avoided; yet where due, they are not to be neglected.

Rule 26a

In pulling off your hat to persons of distinction, as noblemen, justices, and churchmen, make a reverence, bowing more or less according to the custom of the better bred and quality of the person.

Rule 26b

Among your equals, expect not always that they should begin with you first, but to pull off the hat when there is no need is affectation. In the manner of saluting and resaluting in words, keep to the most usual custom.

Rule 27a

Tis ill manners to bid one more eminent than yourself be covered as well as not to do it to whom it is due. Likewise, he that makes too much haste to put on his hat does not well, yet he ought to put it on at the first, or at most the second time of being asked.

Rule 27b

Now what is herein spoken, of qualification in behavior in saluting, ought to be observed in taking of place and sitting down for ceremonies without bounds is troublesome.